T0353695

TILTED CROWN
BOOK OF
AFFIRMATIONS

VOLUME I

AARON L LLOYD II

BALBOA.PRESS
A DIVISION OF HAY HOUSE

Balboa Press books may be ordered through booksellers or by contacting:

Balboa Press
A Division of Hay House
1663 Liberty Drive
Bloomington, IN 47403
www.balboapress.com
844-682-1282

Because of the dynamic nature of the Internet, any web addresses or links contained in this book may have changed since publication and may no longer be valid. The views expressed in this work are solely those of the author and do not necessarily reflect the views of the publisher, and the publisher hereby disclaims any responsibility for them.

The author of this book does not dispense medical advice or prescribe the use of any technique as a form of treatment for physical, emotional, or medical problems without the advice of a physician, either directly or indirectly. The intent of the author is only to offer information of a general nature to help you in your quest for emotional and spiritual well-being. In the event you use any of the information in this book for yourself, which is your constitutional right, the author and the publisher assume no responsibility for your actions.

Any people depicted in stock imagery provided by Getty Images are models, and such images are being used for illustrative purposes only. Certain stock imagery © Getty Images.

Print information available on the last page.

ISBN: 979-8-7652-5827-9 (sc)
ISBN: 979-8-7652-5828-6 (hc)
ISBN: 979-8-7652-5826-2 (e)

Library of Congress Control Number: 2024926114

Balboa Press rev. date: 01/28/2025

LIST OF GOALS

LIST OF GOALS

_____

_____

_____

_____

_____

_____

_____

_____

_____

_____

_____

_____

_____

_____

_____

_____

_____

_____

_____

_____

_____

_____

LIST OF GOALS

_____

_____

_____

_____

_____

_____

_____

_____

_____

_____

_____

_____

_____

_____

_____

_____

_____

_____

_____

_____

_____

_____

_____

_____

_____

_____

I am worthy of respect and love.

I deserves kindness, appreciation, and acceptance simply for being who I am.

Respect and love are fundamental human needs that contribute to our well-being and self-esteem. By acknowledging my worthiness, I cultivate self-confidence and foster healthier relationships. This affirmation encourages me to set boundaries, seek out supportive connections, and embrace my individuality, reinforcing the belief that I am deserving of positive treatment from myself and others. Ultimately, it empowers me to live authentically and pursue fulfilling relationships based on mutual respect and love.

I embrace challenges as opportunities for growth.

Challenges are a natural part of life and often serve as catalysts for personal development. By reframing challenges in this way, I can cultivate resilience, adaptability, and problem-solving skills.

This mindset encourages me to step outside my comfort zones, face fears, and learn valuable lessons from experiences, even when they are difficult. Embracing challenges fosters a growth mindset, allowing me to see setbacks as steppingstones to success rather than failures. Ultimately, this affirmation empowers me to approach life's difficulties with courage and optimism, leading to greater self-discovery and achievement.

I am capable of achieving my dreams.

I have the strength, resources, and determination needed to pursue my aspirations.

By embracing this affirmation, I cultivate self-confidence and motivation, which are essential for overcoming obstacles and taking actionable steps toward my goals. It encourages a proactive mindset, prompting me to set clear objectives, create plans, and persist despite challenges.

Believing in my capability fosters resilience and a sense of purpose, empowering me to turn my dreams into reality. Ultimately, this affirmation reinforces the idea that with dedication and effort, I can achieve my visions and aspirations.

My potential is limitless.

By embracing this belief, I am empowered to pursue my passions, explore new opportunities, and push beyond my comfort zones. It fosters a sense of curiosity and resilience, motivating me to take risks and embrace challenges as I strive for my goals.

Recognizing that potential is limitless helps combat feelings of inadequacy and fear of failure, reinforcing the understanding that growth is a lifelong journey. Ultimately, this affirmation inspires confidence, creativity, and the belief that I can achieve extraordinary things.

I choose to be positive and optimistic.

This choice allows me to focus on the good in every situation, which helps me navigate challenges with resilience. By adopting a positive attitude, I cultivate hope and motivation, making it easier to pursue my goals and overcome obstacles.

Being optimistic also enhances my relationships, as I attract positive energy and support from others. It empowers me to see setbacks as opportunities for growth rather than failures. Ultimately, this choice transforms my perspective, allowing me to approach life with gratitude and enthusiasm, leading to a more fulfilling and joyful existence.

I am confident in my abilities.

I affirm my trust in myself and my skills. This confidence empowers me to tackle challenges and pursue my goals without hesitation. By recognizing my strengths and past accomplishments, I build a solid foundation that reinforces my self-belief.

Being confident allows me to take risks and step out of my comfort zone, knowing that I can handle whatever comes my way. It helps me approach new opportunities with enthusiasm rather than fear, fostering a growth mindset. Ultimately, this belief in my abilities not only enhances my performance but also inspires others around me, creating a positive and encouraging environment for growth and success.

I am proud of who I am becoming.

I celebrate my journey of growth and self-discovery. This affirmation reminds me to recognize the progress I've made and the challenges I've overcome. It encourages me to embrace my evolving identity and appreciate the lessons learned along the way.

Being proud of myself fosters a sense of self-worth and motivates me to continue pursuing my goals with passion and purpose. It helps me stay focused on my values and aspirations, reinforcing the idea that personal growth is a lifelong process. Ultimately, this pride empowers me to embrace my uniqueness and encourages me to keep striving to be the best version of myself.

I attract success and positivity.

I affirm my belief that my mindset and energy draw in positive experiences and opportunities. By cultivating a positive attitude and focusing on my goals, I create an environment that fosters success. This mindset allows me to recognize and seize opportunities that align with my aspirations.

Embracing this affirmation encourages me to surround myself with supportive people and maintain a hopeful outlook, which further amplifies the positive energy in my life. I understand that my thoughts and actions play a crucial role in shaping my reality, and by projecting confidence and optimism, I invite success into my life. Ultimately, this belief empowers me to take proactive steps toward my dreams, reinforcing the idea that I am deserving of all the good things that come my way.

I am strong, both mentally and physically.

I affirm my resilience and capability in all aspects of my life. This belief empowers me to face challenges with courage and determination, knowing that I can handle whatever comes my way.

My mental strength allows me to stay focused, adapt to change, and overcome obstacles, while my physical strength enables me to take action and pursue my goals actively. Recognizing my strength helps me build confidence and encourages me to prioritize self-care, ensuring that I nurture both my body and mind.

Ultimately, this affirmation reinforces my belief in my abilities, reminding me that I am equipped to thrive and that my strength is a vital part of my journey toward success and fulfillment.

I embrace my unique qualities.

When I say, "I embrace my unique qualities," I acknowledge that my individuality is what makes me special. This affirmation allows me to celebrate the traits, experiences, and perspectives that set me apart from others. By valuing my uniqueness, I cultivate self-acceptance and confidence, which helps me navigate life authentically.

Embracing my unique qualities encourages me to express myself freely and pursue my passions without fear of judgment. It also fosters a deeper appreciation for diversity, both in myself and in others. Recognizing that my differences contribute to my strengths empowers me to share my gifts with the world.

Ultimately, this belief reinforces the idea that my uniqueness is not only valuable but essential to my personal growth and the positive impact I can have on those around me. Do you find it easy to embrace your unique qualities, or are there aspects you struggle with?

I am a problem solver.

This belief empowers me to approach obstacles with creativity and determination, knowing that I have the skills to find effective solutions.

Being a problem solver encourages me to stay calm under pressure and think critically about the situation at hand. I recognize that every challenge is an opportunity for growth and learning, and I embrace the process of exploring different perspectives and strategies.

Ultimately, this affirmation boosts my confidence and resilience, reminding me that I have the resourcefulness to overcome difficulties and the mindset to turn challenges into steppingstones on my journey to success.

I learn from my mistakes.

I acknowledge that errors are a natural part of growth and self-improvement. This belief allows me to view setbacks not as failures, but as valuable lessons that contribute to my development.

By embracing my mistakes, I cultivate a mindset of resilience and curiosity, encouraging me to reflect on what went wrong and how I can do better next time. This process helps me build problem-solving skills and increases my confidence in navigating future challenges.

Ultimately, this affirmation empowers me to take risks and pursue my goals without fear, knowing that each misstep brings me one step closer to success and greater understanding of myself.

I radiate positivity and enthusiasm.

I affirm my commitment to approaching life with an optimistic and energetic attitude. This belief inspires me to cultivate a mindset that not only uplifts my own spirit but also influences those around me.

By embracing positivity, I create an environment where encouragement and motivation thrive, attracting like-minded individuals and fostering meaningful connections. My enthusiasm fuels my passion and drives me to pursue my goals with vigor, making challenges feel more manageable and opportunities more exciting.

Ultimately, this affirmation reminds me that my energy can have a powerful impact on my experiences and the people I interact with, encouraging a cycle of positivity that enhances my life and the lives of others.

I am open to new experiences.

I affirm my willingness to embrace change and explore the unknown. This mindset encourages me to step outside my comfort zone, which leads to personal growth and new opportunities.

Being open to new experiences allows me to expand my horizons, meet diverse people, and learn from different perspectives. It fosters a sense of curiosity and adventure, making life more enriching and fulfilling.

Ultimately, this affirmation empowers me to face challenges with a positive attitude, knowing that each new experience contributes to my journey and helps me become a more well-rounded individual.

I respect myself and others.

I affirm the importance of valuing both my own worth and the worth of those around me. This belief encourages me to set healthy boundaries, practice self-care, and honor my own needs and feelings.

By respecting others, I foster empathy and understanding, which enhances my relationships and creates a supportive environment. This mutual respect promotes open communication and collaboration, allowing us to learn from one another.

Ultimately, this affirmation reinforces my commitment to treating myself and others with kindness and dignity, contributing to a more positive and harmonious life.

I am in control of my thoughts and emotions.

I affirm my ability to manage my mental and emotional responses. This belief empowers me to recognize that I have the power to choose how I react to situations, rather than being swept away by my feelings or negative thoughts.

By practicing mindfulness and self-awareness, I can identify unhelpful patterns and replace them with more constructive perspectives. This control enhances my resilience, allowing me to navigate challenges with clarity and composure.

Ultimately, this affirmation reinforces my commitment to emotional well-being, helping me create a more positive and balanced life where I can respond thoughtfully to whatever comes my way.

I have the power to create my own reality.

I affirm my ability to shape my life through my thoughts, actions, and choices. This belief empowers me to take responsibility for my circumstances and recognize that I can influence my future.

By focusing on my goals and aligning my actions with my values, I can manifest the life I desire. This mindset encourages me to overcome obstacles and maintain a positive outlook, knowing that my intentions play a crucial role in my experiences.

Ultimately, this affirmation reinforces my sense of agency and purpose, reminding me that I am the architect of my life and that I have the power to turn my dreams into reality.

I am deserving of happiness and fulfillment.

I affirm my inherent right to experience joy and satisfaction in life. This belief allows me to prioritize my well-being and pursue what truly brings me happiness without guilt or hesitation.

By recognizing my worth, I create space for positive experiences and meaningful relationships. This mindset encourages me to set healthy boundaries and seek out opportunities that align with my passions and values.

Ultimately, this affirmation empowers me to embrace the pursuit of my dreams, reinforcing the understanding that I have every right to lead a fulfilling and joyful life.

I cultivate meaningful relationships.

I affirm my commitment to nurturing connections that enrich my life. This belief encourages me to invest time and effort into building genuine bonds with others, fostering trust, understanding, and support.

By prioritizing meaningful relationships, I create a network of positivity that enhances my well-being and encourages personal growth. I actively seek to communicate openly, listen empathetically, and engage authentically with those around me.

Ultimately, this affirmation reinforces the importance of community and connection, reminding me that the quality of my relationships significantly contributes to my happiness and fulfillment in life.

I face my fears with courage.

I affirm my willingness to confront the challenges that hold me back. This belief empowers me to recognize that fear is a natural part of growth and that overcoming it is essential for my personal development.

By facing my fears, I build resilience and confidence, proving to myself that I can handle difficult situations. This mindset encourages me to step outside my comfort zone and embrace new opportunities, knowing that each courageous act brings me closer to my goals.

Ultimately, this affirmation reinforces my commitment to living authentically and fearlessly, reminding me that I have the strength to transform my fears into steppingstones for success.

I am a lifelong learner.

I affirm my commitment to continuous growth and development throughout my life. This belief inspires me to seek knowledge and new skills in various areas, recognizing that learning is a journey, not a destination.

By embracing the mindset of a lifelong learner, I remain curious and open to new ideas, experiences, and perspectives. This approach helps me adapt to change and challenges, fostering resilience and creativity in my personal and professional life.

Ultimately, this affirmation reinforces my passion for exploration and self-improvement, reminding me that every experience is an opportunity to learn and evolve, enriching my life and the lives of those around me.

I prioritize my mental and physical health.

I affirm my commitment to taking care of myself holistically. This belief encourages me to recognize the importance of maintaining a healthy balance in my life, as both my mind and body are vital to my overall well-being.

By prioritizing my mental health, I engage in practices like mindfulness, self-reflection, and seeking support when needed. Simultaneously, I focus on my physical health through regular exercise, nutritious eating, and sufficient rest.

Ultimately, this affirmation reinforces my understanding that taking care of myself empowers me to live fully and vibrantly, enabling me to pursue my goals and cultivate meaningful relationships with others.

I am resilient in the face of adversity.

I affirm my ability to bounce back from challenges and setbacks. This belief empowers me to view difficulties as opportunities for growth rather than insurmountable obstacles.

By embracing resilience, I develop a mindset that allows me to stay focused and maintain hope, even in tough times. I learn to adapt, problem-solve, and find strength within myself to persevere.

Ultimately, this affirmation reinforces my confidence in my capacity to overcome adversity, reminding me that each challenge I face contributes to my personal growth and strengthens my resolve to move forward.

I believe in my dreams and pursue them passionately.

I affirm my commitment to following my aspirations with enthusiasm and dedication. This belief empowers me to envision a future that aligns with my passions and values, motivating me to act toward achieving my goals.

By believing in my dreams, I cultivate the confidence to overcome obstacles and stay focused on my path, even when challenges arise. My passion fuels my perseverance, driving me to put in the necessary effort and remain resilient in the face of setbacks.

Ultimately, this affirmation reinforces my understanding that my dreams are worth pursuing and that my commitment to them can lead to a fulfilling and meaningful life.

I am grateful for my journey.

I affirm my appreciation for all the experiences—both positive and challenging—that have shaped who I am today. This belief encourages me to reflect on the lessons I've learned and the growth I've experienced along the way.

By embracing gratitude for my journey, I cultivate a positive mindset that allows me to see value in every step I take. It reminds me to celebrate my accomplishments and acknowledge the resilience I've built through adversity.

Ultimately, this affirmation reinforces my understanding that my journey is unique and meaningful, guiding me toward a future filled with hope and possibility.

I can adapt to any situation.

I affirm my ability to remain flexible and open-minded in the face of change. This belief empowers me to approach challenges with confidence, knowing that I can adjust my mindset and strategies as needed.

By embracing adaptability, I cultivate resilience and resourcefulness, allowing me to navigate unexpected circumstances and thrive in diverse environments. This mindset encourages me to view change as an opportunity for growth rather than a setback.

Ultimately, this affirmation reinforces my understanding that I have the strength and skills to handle whatever life throws my way, enabling me to move forward with assurance and optimism.

I am a positive influence on others.

I affirm my commitment to uplifting those around me through my actions and attitude. This belief empowers me to create a supportive and encouraging environment, where my energy can inspire growth and motivation in others.

By embodying positivity, I cultivate meaningful connections and foster an atmosphere of collaboration and trust. I recognize that my words and behavior can have a significant impact, encouraging others to pursue their goals and embrace their own potential.

Ultimately, this affirmation reinforces my understanding that my influence can contribute to the well-being and success of others, reminding me that I have the power to make a difference in their lives.

I trust my intuition.

I affirm my belief in my inner wisdom and gut feelings. This trust empowers me to listen to my instincts and make decisions that align with my true self, even in uncertain situations.

By honoring my intuition, I cultivate self-awareness and confidence in my choices. This belief encourages me to reflect on my experiences and emotions, guiding me toward paths that resonate with my values and aspirations.

Ultimately, this affirmation reinforces my understanding that my intuition is a valuable tool in navigating life, helping me to embrace opportunities and challenges with clarity and assurance.

I am focused and determined.

I affirm my commitment to staying on track toward my goals. This belief empowers me to concentrate my energy and attention on what truly matters, minimizing distractions along the way.

By embracing focus and determination, I cultivate a strong sense of purpose that drives me to take consistent action. This mindset helps me overcome obstacles and maintain motivation, even when faced with challenges.

Ultimately, this affirmation reinforces my understanding that with clarity and resolve, I can achieve my aspirations and turn my dreams into reality.

I forgive myself and others.

I affirm my commitment to releasing resentment and embracing healing. This belief empowers me to let go of past mistakes, recognizing that holding onto grudges only hinders my growth and happiness.

By practicing forgiveness, I free myself from negative emotions and create space for compassion and understanding. This mindset allows me to move forward with a lighter heart, strengthening my relationships and fostering a sense of peace.

Ultimately, this affirmation reinforces my understanding that forgiveness is a powerful tool for personal well-being, enabling me to cultivate healthier connections with myself and those around me.

I take pride in my accomplishments.

I affirm my recognition of the hard work and dedication that have led me to where I am today. This belief encourages me to celebrate my achievements, both big and small, and acknowledge the effort I put into reaching my goals.

By taking pride in my accomplishments, I boost my self-confidence and motivate myself to pursue new challenges. This mindset helps me reflect on my journey and appreciate the progress I've made, reinforcing my belief in my capabilities.

Ultimately, this affirmation reminds me that honoring my achievements fosters a positive self-image and inspires me to continue striving for success in all areas of my life.

I embrace change with an open heart.

I affirm my willingness to welcome new experiences and opportunities. This belief empowers me to view change not as a threat, but as a chance for growth and discovery.

By embracing change, I cultivate resilience and adaptability, allowing me to navigate life's transitions with grace and positivity. This mindset encourages me to stay curious and open-minded, fostering a sense of adventure in my journey.

Ultimately, this affirmation reinforces my understanding that change is a natural part of life, and by approaching it with an open heart, I can create space for new possibilities and deeper connections.

I communicate effectively and assertively.

I affirm my ability to express my thoughts and feelings clearly while respecting myself and others. This belief empowers me to engage in honest and open dialogue, fostering understanding and connection in my relationships.

By communicating assertively, I build confidence in sharing my needs and boundaries without fear. This approach helps me navigate conversations with empathy and clarity, allowing for constructive interactions.

Ultimately, this affirmation reinforces my understanding that effective communication is key to building healthy relationships and achieving my goals, enabling me to connect with others in a meaningful way.

I am surrounded by love and support.

I affirm my awareness of the positive relationships and connections in my life. This belief empowers me to recognize the care and encouragement I receive from family, friends, and my community.

By embracing this affirmation, I cultivate gratitude for the people who uplift me and remind me that I am never alone. This mindset helps me feel more secure and confident, knowing I have a network of support to turn to during both challenges and triumphs.

Ultimately, this affirmation reinforces my understanding that love and support are essential to my well-being, allowing me to thrive and pursue my goals with the assurance that I have a strong foundation behind me.

I am making progress every day.

I affirm my commitment to personal growth and self-improvement. This belief encourages me to recognize that even small steps contribute to my overall journey, reminding me that progress is not always linear but still valuable.

By focusing on my daily achievements, I build motivation and confidence in my abilities. This mindset helps me celebrate my efforts, no matter how minor they may seem, reinforcing the idea that every action brings me closer to my goals.

Ultimately, this affirmation reinforces my understanding that progress is a continuous process, and by acknowledging my daily growth, I empower myself to keep moving forward with purpose and determination.

I choose to let go of negativity.

I affirm my decision to release unhelpful thoughts and emotions that no longer serve me. This belief empowers me to create space for positivity and growth in my life, allowing me to focus on what truly matters.

By letting go of negativity, I free myself from unnecessary stress and resentment, fostering a more optimistic mindset. This choice encourages me to seek out uplifting experiences and surround myself with supportive people, enhancing my overall well-being.

Ultimately, this affirmation reinforces my understanding that letting go of negativity is an active process that enables me to live more fully and authentically, paving the way for a brighter and more fulfilling future.

I celebrate my successes, big and small.

I affirm my commitment to recognizing and appreciating my achievements. This belief empowers me to acknowledge the effort I've put into reaching my goals, no matter the size of the accomplishment.

By celebrating my successes, I cultivate a sense of gratitude and self-worth, reinforcing my motivation to continue pursuing my dreams. This mindset helps me stay positive and inspired, reminding me that every step forward is worth recognizing.

Ultimately, this affirmation reinforces my understanding that celebrating my successes contributes to my overall happiness and encourages me to keep striving for growth and fulfillment in my life.

I am patient with myself and my growth.

I affirm my understanding that personal development is a journey that takes time. This belief empowers me to recognize that setbacks and challenges are a natural part of the process, allowing me to treat myself with kindness and compassion.

By practicing patience, I give myself the grace to learn and evolve at my own pace, reducing self-judgment and frustration. This mindset encourages me to celebrate my progress, no matter how small, and to remain committed to my goals without the pressure of immediate results.

Ultimately, this affirmation reinforces my understanding that patience is essential for sustainable growth, helping me cultivate a healthier relationship with myself as I continue to move forward on my journey.

I am worthy of success and abundance.

I affirm my belief in my inherent value and the right to achieve my goals. This belief empowers me to embrace opportunities and pursue my aspirations without guilt or doubt.

By recognizing my worthiness, I create a mindset that attracts positivity and prosperity into my life. This understanding encourages me to take bold actions toward my dreams, reinforcing the idea that I deserve the rewards of my hard work.

Ultimately, this affirmation reinforces my commitment to pursuing success and abundance, reminding me that I am deserving of all the good things that come my way.

I pursue my passions wholeheartedly.

I affirm my commitment to engaging fully in what inspires and excites me. This belief empowers me to prioritize my interests and dedicate time and energy to the activities that bring me joy and fulfillment.

By embracing my passions, I cultivate a sense of purpose and motivation that fuels my personal growth. This mindset encourages me to explore new opportunities and embrace creativity, enriching my life with meaningful experiences.

Ultimately, this affirmation reinforces my understanding that pursuing my passions is essential for my happiness and well-being, allowing me to live authentically and with intention.

I am not afraid to ask for help.

I affirm my understanding that seeking support is a sign of strength, not weakness. This belief empowers me to recognize that collaboration and guidance can enhance my growth and well-being.

By being open to asking for help, I cultivate stronger connections with others and create opportunities for learning and shared experiences. This mindset encourages me to overcome the fear of vulnerability and embrace the support available to me.

Ultimately, this affirmation reinforces my understanding that reaching out for help is a valuable part of my journey, enabling me to navigate challenges more effectively and foster a sense of community.

I live with integrity and honesty.

I affirm my commitment to being true to myself and my values. This belief empowers me to act consistently, ensuring that my words and actions align with my principles.

By embracing integrity and honesty, I cultivate trust in my relationships and foster an authentic connection with others. This mindset encourages me to make choices that reflect my core beliefs, even when faced with challenges or temptations.

Ultimately, this affirmation reinforces my understanding that living with integrity is essential for my personal fulfillment and peace of mind, allowing me to navigate life with confidence and authenticity.

I am a beacon of hope and inspiration.

I affirm my ability to uplift and motivate those around me through my actions and attitude. This belief empowers me to recognize the positive impact I can have on others, encouraging them to pursue their own dreams and overcome challenges.

By embodying hope and inspiration, I cultivate an environment where positivity flourishes, fostering resilience and confidence in myself and those I interact with. This mindset encourages me to share my journey and lessons learned, reinforcing the idea that we can all grow and thrive together.

Ultimately, this affirmation reminds me that my presence and energy can light the way for others, allowing me to contribute to a more optimistic and supportive community.

I find joy in the little things.

I affirm my ability to appreciate the simple pleasures in life. This belief empowers me to focus on the present moment and recognize the beauty in everyday experiences, whether it's a warm cup of coffee, a beautiful sunset, or a kind word from a friend.

By embracing this mindset, I cultivate gratitude and positivity, allowing me to enhance my overall well-being. This appreciation for the little things encourages me to slow down and savor life's moments, fostering a deeper sense of fulfillment and happiness.

Ultimately, this affirmation reinforces my understanding that joy can be found all around me, and by acknowledging these small delights, I enrich my life and nurture a more optimistic outlook.

I create my own opportunities.

I affirm my belief in my ability to take initiative and shape my path. This mindset empowers me to recognize that I have the power to pursue my goals actively, rather than waiting for chances to come my way.

By taking proactive steps and being open to new possibilities, I cultivate a sense of agency and resourcefulness. This belief encourages me to explore my interests, network with others, and seek out experiences that align with my aspirations.

Ultimately, this affirmation reinforces my understanding that I am in control of my journey, and by creating my own opportunities, I can build the future I desire and deserve.

I am courageous in the face of challenges.

I affirm my ability to confront difficulties with strength and determination. This belief empowers me to view obstacles as opportunities for growth rather than insurmountable barriers.

By embracing courage, I cultivate resilience and confidence, allowing me to tackle challenges head-on and learn from my experiences. This mindset encourages me to step outside my comfort zone and pursue my goals, even when fear or uncertainty arises.

Ultimately, this affirmation reinforces my understanding that courage is a vital part of my journey, enabling me to navigate life's ups and downs with grace and conviction.

I honor my commitments and responsibilities.

I affirm my dedication to following through on my promises and obligations. This belief empowers me to recognize the importance of accountability and reliability in my personal and professional life.

By honoring my commitments, I build trust with others and strengthen my relationships, knowing that my actions reflect my values. This mindset encourages me to prioritize my responsibilities, ensuring that I contribute positively to the lives of those around me.

Ultimately, this affirmation reinforces my understanding that honoring my commitments fosters a sense of integrity and fulfillment, allowing me to live authentically and make a meaningful impact in my community.

I embrace my emotions and express them healthily.

I affirm my commitment to acknowledging and understanding my feelings. This belief empowers me to accept my emotions without judgment, recognizing that they are a natural part of being human.

By embracing my emotions, I create space for self-reflection and growth, allowing me to express myself in constructive ways. This mindset encourages me to communicate my feelings openly and seek support when needed, fostering healthier relationships with myself and others.

Ultimately, this affirmation reinforces my understanding that expressing my emotions healthily contributes to my overall well-being and enhances my ability to navigate life's challenges with authenticity and clarity.

I am building a bright future for myself.

I affirm my commitment to taking positive actions that shape my desired outcomes. This belief empowers me to set clear goals and take deliberate steps toward achieving them, recognizing that my efforts today lay the foundation for tomorrow.

By focusing on my aspirations, I cultivate a sense of purpose and motivation that drives me to make choices aligned with my values and dreams. This mindset encourages me to embrace opportunities for growth and learning, reinforcing my confidence in my ability to create the life I envision.

Ultimately, this affirmation reinforces my understanding that I have the power to design my future, and by actively working toward my goals, I am paving the way for a fulfilling and successful life.

I attract positive energy into my life.

I affirm my ability to create an environment filled with optimism and joy. This belief empowers me to cultivate a mindset that focuses on the good in myself and others, drawing in uplifting experiences and relationships.

By radiating positivity, I open myself up to new opportunities and connections that enhance my well-being. This mindset encourages me to engage in practices that nurture my spirit, such as gratitude and mindfulness, further amplifying the positive energy I attract.

Ultimately, this affirmation reinforces my understanding that the energy I project influences my surroundings, and by fostering positivity within myself, I can create a life rich with happiness and fulfillment.

I value my time and use it wisely.

I affirm my commitment to making conscious choices about how I spend my days. This belief empowers me to prioritize activities that align with my goals and values, ensuring that I invest my time in what truly matters.

By valuing my time, I cultivate a sense of purpose and focus, helping me avoid distractions and procrastination. This mindset encourages me to set boundaries and allocate time for self-care, growth, and meaningful connections.

Ultimately, this affirmation reinforces my understanding that time is a precious resource, and by using it wisely, I can create a fulfilling and productive life that reflects my aspirations and desires.

I am a work in progress, and that's okay.

I affirm my understanding that growth and self-improvement are ongoing journeys. This belief empowers me to embrace my imperfections and recognize that it's natural to evolve over time.

By accepting that I am a work in progress, I cultivate patience and compassion for myself, allowing me to celebrate small victories and learn from setbacks. This mindset encourages me to focus on continuous learning and development rather than striving for perfection.

Ultimately, this affirmation reinforces my understanding that every step I take, no matter how small, contributes to my personal growth and that it's perfectly okay to be on this journey of becoming.

I celebrate my individuality.

I affirm my appreciation for what makes me unique. This belief empowers me to embrace my distinct qualities, experiences, and perspectives, recognizing that they contribute to my identity and enrich my life.

By celebrating my individuality, I cultivate self-acceptance and confidence, allowing me to express myself authentically without fear of judgment. This mindset encourages me to honor my preferences and passions, fostering a deeper connection with myself and others.

Ultimately, this affirmation reinforces my understanding that my individuality is a strength, and by embracing it, I can inspire others to do the same, creating a vibrant and diverse community.

I make decisions that align with my values.

I affirm my commitment to living authentically and true to myself. This belief empowers me to prioritize my principles when faced with choices, ensuring that my actions reflect what truly matters to me.

By aligning my decisions with my values, I cultivate a sense of integrity and purpose, which enhances my overall well-being. This mindset encourages me to evaluate options carefully, allowing me to choose paths that resonate with my beliefs and aspirations.

Ultimately, this affirmation reinforces my understanding that making value-driven decisions leads to a more fulfilling life, helping me to create a reality that aligns with who I am and what I stand for.

I take risks that lead to personal growth.

I affirm my willingness to step outside my comfort zone and embrace new experiences. This belief empowers me to recognize that growth often comes from taking chances and facing the unknown.

By taking calculated risks, I challenge myself to expand my horizons and learn valuable lessons along the way. This mindset encourages me to view failures as opportunities for growth rather than setbacks, fostering resilience and adaptability.

Ultimately, this affirmation reinforces my understanding that taking risks is an essential part of my journey, helping me to develop new skills, discover my potential, and enrich my life in meaningful ways.

I am deserving of love and companionship.

I affirm my inherent worth and the right to meaningful connections with others. This belief empowers me to recognize that I am worthy of affection, support, and healthy relationships.

By embracing my deservingness, I open myself up to receiving love and companionship, allowing me to build deeper connections with those around me. This mindset encourages me to nurture my relationships and seek out environments that foster genuine connection and understanding.

Ultimately, this affirmation reinforces my understanding that love and companionship are vital to my well-being, and by acknowledging my worthiness, I can cultivate fulfilling relationships that enrich my life.

I stand up for what I believe in.

I affirm my commitment to advocating for my values and principles. This belief empowers me to express my thoughts and opinions confidently, even when faced with opposition or challenges.

By standing up for my beliefs, I cultivate a sense of integrity and self-respect, knowing that I am true to myself. This mindset encourages me to engage in meaningful discussions and contribute positively to the issues I care about, fostering a sense of community and shared purpose.

Ultimately, this affirmation reinforces my understanding that taking a stand is essential for personal fulfillment and social change, reminding me that my voice matters and can make a difference.

I have a unique purpose in life.

I affirm my belief that I am here for a reason, with distinct gifts and contributions to offer the world. This belief empowers me to explore my passions and interests, helping me uncover what truly inspires me.

By recognizing my unique purpose, I cultivate a sense of direction and motivation, guiding my choices and actions. This mindset encourages me to embrace my individuality and pursue paths that align with my values and aspirations.

Ultimately, this affirmation reinforces my understanding that my life has significance, and by honoring my unique purpose, I can make a meaningful impact on myself and those around me.

I am kind to myself and others.

I affirm my commitment to fostering compassion and understanding in my interactions. This belief empowers me to treat myself with the same kindness I offer to those around me, recognizing that self-compassion is essential for my well-being.

By practicing kindness, I create a positive environment that nurtures connection and support. This mindset encourages me to be empathetic, patient, and forgiving, both toward myself and others, allowing for deeper, more meaningful relationships.

Ultimately, this affirmation reinforces my understanding that kindness is a powerful force that enhances my life and the lives of those I encounter, helping to create a more loving and supportive world.

I choose to see the good in every situation.

I affirm my commitment to maintaining a positive outlook, even during challenging times. This belief empowers me to look for the silver linings and lessons in every experience, allowing me to grow and adapt.

By choosing to focus on the good, I cultivate resilience and optimism, which helps me navigate difficulties with a balanced perspective. This mindset encourages me to approach life with gratitude and hope, fostering a sense of peace and contentment.

Ultimately, this affirmation reinforces my understanding that my perspective shapes my experiences, and by choosing to see the good, I can create a more fulfilling and joyful life.

I am committed to self-improvement.

I affirm my dedication to growing and evolving in all areas of my life. This belief empowers me to seek out new knowledge, skills, and experiences that enhance my personal and professional development.

By prioritizing self-improvement, I cultivate a mindset of curiosity and resilience, embracing challenges as opportunities to learn and grow. This commitment encourages me to set meaningful goals and take consistent action toward achieving them.

Ultimately, this affirmation reinforces my understanding that self-improvement is a lifelong journey, and by being dedicated to my growth, I can create a more fulfilling and enriched life.

I express gratitude daily.

I affirm my commitment to recognizing and appreciating the positive aspects of my life. This belief empowers me to focus on what I have rather than what I lack, fostering a sense of contentment and joy.

By practicing daily gratitude, I cultivate a positive mindset that enhances my overall well-being and helps me navigate challenges with resilience. This mindset encourages me to acknowledge even the small blessings, deepening my appreciation for the people and experiences that enrich my life.

Ultimately, this affirmation reinforces my understanding that expressing gratitude is a powerful practice that brings more positivity into my life and strengthens my connections with others.

I am a source of strength for those around me.

I affirm my ability to support and uplift others through my actions and presence. This belief empowers me to recognize the positive impact I can have on friends, family, and my community.

By being a source of strength, I cultivate empathy and compassion, allowing me to offer encouragement and understanding during difficult times. This mindset encourages me to lead by example, showing resilience and positivity that inspire others to overcome their challenges.

Ultimately, this affirmation reinforces my understanding that my strength can create a ripple effect, helping to foster a supportive environment where everyone can thrive and feel valued.

I value honesty and authenticity.

I affirm my commitment to being true to myself and others. This belief empowers me to communicate openly and transparently, fostering trust in my relationships.

By prioritizing honesty and authenticity, I create a foundation of integrity that guides my actions and decisions. This mindset encourages me to embrace vulnerability, allowing me to connect with others on a deeper level and cultivate meaningful relationships.

Ultimately, this affirmation reinforces my understanding that valuing honesty and authenticity not only enriches my life but also inspires those around me to be genuine and true to themselves.

I am capable of overcoming any obstacle.

I affirm my resilience and strength in the face of challenges. This belief empowers me to approach difficulties with confidence, knowing that I have the skills and determination to find solutions.

By embracing this mindset, I cultivate a sense of empowerment that encourages me to tackle obstacles head-on rather than shy away from them. This perspective helps me view setbacks as opportunities for growth and learning, reinforcing my ability to adapt and persevere.

Ultimately, this affirmation reinforces my understanding that I possess the inner strength to navigate life's challenges, and by believing in my capability, I can turn obstacles into steppingstones toward my goals.

I pursue knowledge and understanding.

I affirm my commitment to lifelong learning and personal growth. This belief empowers me to seek out new information, experiences, and perspectives that enrich my life and broaden my horizons.

By actively pursuing knowledge, I cultivate curiosity and critical thinking, allowing me to navigate the world with confidence and insight. This mindset encourages me to engage in discussions, ask questions, and remain open to new ideas, fostering deeper connections with others.

Ultimately, this affirmation reinforces my understanding that knowledge and understanding are essential for my development, enabling me to make informed decisions and contribute positively to my community.

I am proud of my achievements.

I affirm my recognition of the hard work and dedication I've invested in reaching my goals. This belief empowers me to celebrate my successes, no matter how big or small, and acknowledge the effort it took to get there.

By embracing this pride, I cultivate self-confidence and motivation, reinforcing my belief in my abilities. This mindset encourages me to reflect on my journey and appreciate the progress I've made, which fuels my desire to continue striving for future accomplishments.

Ultimately, this affirmation reinforces my understanding that taking pride in my achievements is essential for my personal growth and fulfillment, reminding me that I am capable of achieving great things.

I listen to my inner voice.

I affirm my commitment to tuning into my intuition and instincts. This belief empowers me to trust myself and make decisions that resonate with my true values and desires.

By prioritizing my inner voice, I cultivate self-awareness and clarity, allowing me to navigate life's choices with confidence. This mindset encourages me to reflect on my feelings and thoughts, ensuring that I stay aligned with what truly matters to me.

Ultimately, this affirmation reinforces my understanding that listening to my inner voice is essential for living authentically and making choices that lead to fulfillment and happiness.

I am open to feedback and growth.

I affirm my willingness to embrace constructive criticism and learn from others. This belief empowers me to view feedback as an opportunity for improvement rather than a setback.

By being open to feedback, I cultivate a mindset of continuous learning and development, allowing me to enhance my skills and understanding. This openness encourages me to engage in meaningful conversations and foster stronger relationships, as I recognize the value of diverse perspectives.

Ultimately, this affirmation reinforces my understanding that being receptive to feedback is essential for my personal and professional growth, enabling me to evolve and become the best version of myself.

I create balance in my life.

I affirm my commitment to managing my time and energy effectively across various aspects of my life. This belief empowers me to prioritize what truly matters, ensuring that I dedicate attention to work, relationships, self-care, and personal interests.

By focusing on balance, I cultivate a sense of harmony that reduces stress and enhances my overall well-being. This mindset encourages me to set boundaries and make mindful choices, allowing me to enjoy each moment fully without feeling overwhelmed.

Ultimately, this affirmation reinforces my understanding that creating balance is essential for a fulfilling life, enabling me to thrive in all areas while maintaining a sense of peace and contentment.

I am a positive force in my community.

I affirm my commitment to making a meaningful impact on those around me. This belief empowers me to engage actively and contribute in ways that uplift and support others.

By being a positive force, I cultivate a sense of connection and responsibility, encouraging collaboration and kindness within my community. This mindset motivates me to share my skills, knowledge, and resources, fostering an environment of encouragement and growth.

Ultimately, this affirmation reinforces my understanding that my actions can inspire change and create a ripple effect, helping to build a stronger, more supportive community for everyone.

I am not defined by my past.

I affirm my belief in my ability to grow and evolve beyond previous experiences. This belief empowers me to recognize that my past does not dictate my future; instead, it serves as a foundation for learning and growth.

By embracing this mindset, I cultivate resilience and self-acceptance, allowing me to let go of regrets and embrace new possibilities. This perspective encourages me to focus on the present and the choices I can make today to shape my future.

Ultimately, this affirmation reinforces my understanding that I am in control of my narrative, and by choosing to move forward with purpose, I can create a life that reflects my true self and aspirations.

I strive for excellence in everything I do.

I affirm my commitment to putting forth my best effort in all areas of my life. This belief empowers me to set high standards for myself, motivating me to continuously improve and grow.

By striving for excellence, I cultivate a sense of pride and fulfillment in my accomplishments, knowing that I am dedicated to achieving my goals. This mindset encourages me to embrace challenges and seek opportunities for learning, pushing me to reach my full potential.

Ultimately, this affirmation reinforces my understanding that pursuing excellence not only enhances my own life but also inspires those around me to elevate their own efforts, creating a positive ripple effect in my community.

I take responsibility for my actions.

I affirm my commitment to accountability and integrity in my life. This belief empowers me to own my choices and their consequences, recognizing that I have the power to influence my circumstances.

By taking responsibility, I cultivate self-awareness and growth, allowing me to learn from my mistakes and make better decisions in the future. This mindset encourages me to approach challenges with a proactive attitude, focusing on solutions rather than blaming external factors.

Ultimately, this affirmation reinforces my understanding that taking responsibility is essential for personal growth and building trust in my relationships, enabling me to lead a more authentic and fulfilling life.

I treat myself with kindness and compassion.

I affirm my commitment to nurturing my own well-being. This belief empowers me to recognize my worth and extend the same understanding and care to myself that I offer to others.

By practicing kindness and compassion toward myself, I cultivate a positive self-image and emotional resilience, allowing me to navigate challenges with greater ease. This mindset encourages me to embrace my imperfections and to prioritize self-care, fostering a healthier relationship with myself.

Ultimately, this affirmation reinforces my understanding that treating myself with kindness and compassion is essential for my overall happiness and personal growth, enabling me to thrive in all aspects of my life.

I embrace my journey and its lessons.

I affirm my commitment to valuing every experience, both the highs and the lows. This belief empowers me to recognize that each step I take contributes to my growth and understanding of myself and the world.

By embracing my journey, I cultivate resilience and openness, allowing me to learn from challenges and celebrate successes. This mindset encourages me to reflect on my experiences with gratitude, helping me appreciate the wisdom gained along the way.

Ultimately, this affirmation reinforces my understanding that my journey is uniquely mine, and by embracing it fully, I can transform obstacles into valuable lessons that shape my future.

I am worthy of my dreams.

I affirm my belief in my value and potential. This conviction empowers me to pursue my aspirations with confidence, knowing that I have the right to chase what truly fulfills me.

By recognizing my worthiness, I cultivate self-esteem and motivation, allowing me to take bold steps toward achieving my goals. This mindset encourages me to overcome self-doubt and embrace opportunities that align with my dreams.

Ultimately, this affirmation reinforces my understanding that I deserve to pursue my passions and create a life that reflects my true desires, reminding me that my dreams are not just possible but within my reach.

I practice self-discipline and focus.

I affirm my commitment to maintaining control over my actions and thoughts. This belief empowers me to prioritize my goals and stay on track, even when faced with distractions or challenges.

By cultivating self-discipline, I develop the ability to make choices that align with my long-term aspirations, enhancing my productivity and effectiveness. This mindset encourages me to set clear intentions and follow through on my commitments, reinforcing my dedication to personal growth.

Ultimately, this affirmation reinforces my understanding that practicing self-discipline and focus is essential for achieving my dreams, allowing me to create a life of purpose and fulfillment.

I surround myself with positive influences.

I affirm my commitment to creating an uplifting environment that supports my growth and well-being. This belief empowers me to seek out relationships and experiences that inspire and motivate me.

By surrounding myself with positive influences, I cultivate a mindset of encouragement and support, which helps me stay focused on my goals. This mindset encourages me to engage with people who uplift me and foster a sense of community and connection.

Ultimately, this affirmation reinforces my understanding that the energy I bring into my life shapes my experiences, and by choosing positive influences, I create a more fulfilling and joyful existence.

I express my creativity freely.

I affirm my commitment to embracing my unique ideas and talents without fear or hesitation. This belief empowers me to explore my imagination and share my perspectives, knowing that my creativity is valuable and worthy of expression.

By allowing myself to be creative, I cultivate joy and fulfillment, enriching my life and the lives of those around me. This mindset encourages me to take risks and experiment, fostering a sense of playfulness and openness in my endeavors.

Ultimately, this affirmation reinforces my understanding that expressing my creativity is an essential part of who I am, enabling me to connect more deeply with myself and others while contributing positively to the world.

I nurture my mental well-being.

I affirm my commitment to prioritizing my emotional and psychological health. This belief empowers me to engage in practices that support my mental clarity, resilience, and overall happiness.

By nurturing my mental well-being, I cultivate self-awareness and emotional intelligence, allowing me to manage stress and navigate life's challenges more effectively. This mindset encourages me to seek out activities that bring me joy, peace, and fulfillment, such as mindfulness, self-care, and meaningful connections.

Ultimately, this affirmation reinforces my understanding that taking care of my mental well-being is essential for living a balanced and fulfilling life, enabling me to thrive both personally and in my relationships with others.

I am adaptable and resourceful.

I affirm my ability to navigate change and challenges with confidence. This belief empowers me to embrace new situations and find creative solutions, knowing that I can adjust my approach as needed.

By being adaptable, I cultivate resilience and open-mindedness, allowing me to thrive in diverse environments and circumstances. This mindset encourages me to think critically and utilize the resources available to me, transforming obstacles into opportunities for growth.

Ultimately, this affirmation reinforces my understanding that my adaptability and resourcefulness are key strengths, enabling me to face life's uncertainties with a proactive and positive attitude.

I seek solutions rather than dwelling on problems.

I affirm my commitment to a proactive mindset that focuses on finding ways forward. This belief empowers me to approach challenges with a constructive attitude, prioritizing action over inaction.

By seeking solutions, I cultivate resilience and creativity, allowing me to think critically and explore various options. This mindset encourages me to shift my perspective from negativity to possibility, fostering a sense of empowerment and hope.

Ultimately, this affirmation reinforces my understanding that focusing on solutions enables me to navigate obstacles effectively, turning challenges into opportunities for growth and learning in my life.

I am grateful for my strengths.

I affirm my appreciation for the unique qualities and abilities that define who I am. This belief empowers me to recognize the value I bring to my life and the lives of others, fostering a sense of self-worth and confidence.

By acknowledging my strengths, I cultivate a positive self-image that encourages me to leverage these abilities in pursuit of my goals. This mindset helps me navigate challenges with resilience, knowing I have the tools to overcome obstacles.

Ultimately, this affirmation reinforces my understanding that gratitude for my strengths not only enhances my personal growth but also inspires me to use my talents to contribute positively to the world around me.

I trust the timing of my life.

I affirm my belief in the natural flow of my journey and the importance of patience. This belief empowers me to let go of anxiety about when things should happen and to embrace each moment as it comes.

By trusting the timing of my life, I cultivate a sense of peace and acceptance, allowing me to focus on my growth rather than rushing toward outcomes. This mindset encourages me to recognize that each experience contributes to my overall path and that everything unfolds in its own time.

Ultimately, this affirmation reinforces my understanding that trusting the timing of my life helps me navigate challenges with grace and confidence, reminding me that I am exactly where I need to be on my journey.

I am committed to my goals.

I affirm my dedication to pursuing my aspirations with determination and focus. This belief empowers me to take consistent actions that align with my objectives, reinforcing my resolve to achieve what truly matters to me.

By committing to my goals, I cultivate discipline and motivation, allowing me to overcome obstacles and stay on track even when faced with challenges. This mindset encourages me to set clear intentions and remain accountable to myself, fostering a sense of purpose in my daily life.

Ultimately, this affirmation reinforces my understanding that my commitment to my goals is essential for personal growth and fulfillment, enabling me to turn my dreams into reality and create a life I truly desire.

I cultivate a growth mindset.

I affirm my belief in the power of learning and improvement. This belief empowers me to embrace challenges as opportunities for growth, recognizing that my abilities and intelligence can be developed over time.

By cultivating a growth mindset, I foster resilience and curiosity, allowing me to approach setbacks with a positive attitude and a desire to learn. This mindset encourages me to seek feedback and new experiences, enhancing my skills and expanding my perspective.

Ultimately, this affirmation reinforces my understanding that embracing a growth mindset is essential for my personal and professional development, enabling me to navigate life with confidence and a willingness to evolve.

I value the power of empathy.

I affirm my commitment to understanding and connecting with others on a deeper level. This belief empowers me to recognize the importance of compassion in building strong, meaningful relationships.

By valuing empathy, I cultivate an open heart and mind, allowing me to listen actively and respond thoughtfully to the feelings and experiences of others. This mindset encourages me to create a supportive environment where everyone feels seen and heard.

Ultimately, this affirmation reinforces my understanding that empathy is a powerful tool for fostering connection and healing, enabling me to contribute positively to my community and nurture a sense of belonging.

I honor my body and take care of it.

I affirm my commitment to prioritizing my physical health and well-being. This belief empowers me to recognize that my body is a vital part of who I am, deserving of respect and care.

By honoring my body, I cultivate healthy habits, such as nourishing it with wholesome foods, engaging in regular exercise, and allowing myself adequate rest. This mindset encourages me to listen to my body's needs and respond with kindness and understanding.

Ultimately, this affirmation reinforces my understanding that taking care of my body enhances my overall quality of life, enabling me to feel energized, resilient, and capable of pursuing my goals with confidence.

I embrace my journey.

I affirm my commitment to valuing the unique experiences and lessons that shape my life. This belief empowers me to recognize that each phase of my journey is important for my growth and self-discovery.

By embracing my journey, I cultivate a sense of curiosity and openness, allowing me to learn from challenges and celebrate my achievements. This mindset encourages me to explore new opportunities and connect with others who share similar paths.

Ultimately, this affirmation reinforces my understanding that embracing my journey helps me build resilience and confidence, guiding me toward becoming the person I aspire to be.

I make choices that reflect my values.

I affirm my commitment to living authentically and purposefully. This belief empowers me to evaluate my decisions based on what truly matters to me, ensuring that my actions align with my principles.

By prioritizing my values, I cultivate integrity and self-awareness, allowing me to navigate life's complexities with clarity and confidence. This mindset encourages me to be intentional in my choices, fostering a sense of fulfillment and alignment in my life.

Ultimately, this affirmation reinforces my understanding that making choices that reflect my values is essential for my personal growth and happiness, enabling me to create a life that resonates with who I truly am.

I am surrounded by abundance.

I affirm my belief in the richness of life and the many opportunities available to me. This belief empowers me to recognize the value in my experiences, relationships, and resources, fostering a mindset of gratitude and appreciation.

By embracing the idea of abundance, I cultivate positivity and openness, allowing me to attract more good things into my life. This mindset encourages me to see challenges as opportunities and to appreciate the little joys that enrich my everyday existence.

Ultimately, this affirmation reinforces my understanding that recognizing the abundance around me enhances my overall well-being and helps me create a fulfilling life filled with possibility and joy.

I believe in my ability to inspire others.

I affirm my commitment to using my strengths and experiences to motivate those around me. This belief empowers me to recognize that my actions and words can create a positive impact in the lives of others.

By embracing this mindset, I cultivate confidence and authenticity, allowing me to share my journey and insights openly. This encourages me to lead by example, fostering connections and encouraging others to pursue their own aspirations.

Ultimately, this affirmation reinforces my understanding that believing in my ability to inspire others not only enriches their lives but also deepens my sense of purpose and fulfillment in my own journey.

I practice patience and understanding.

I affirm my commitment to fostering a calm and compassionate approach in my interactions with others and myself. This belief empowers me to recognize that growth and change take time, allowing me to respond thoughtfully rather than react impulsively.

By cultivating patience and understanding, I create space for deeper connections and open communication, enabling me to navigate challenges with grace. This mindset encourages me to appreciate different perspectives and to support others on their journeys without judgment.

Ultimately, this affirmation reinforces my understanding that practicing patience and understanding enriches my relationships and enhances my overall well-being, allowing me to live more harmoniously with myself and those around me.

I am deserving of respect and kindness.

I affirm my inherent worth and value as an individual. This belief empowers me to set healthy boundaries and expect positive treatment from myself and others, reinforcing my self-esteem.

By recognizing my deservingness, I cultivate confidence and assertiveness, allowing me to advocate for my needs and prioritize my well-being. This mindset encourages me to treat myself and others with kindness, creating a supportive environment that fosters mutual respect.

Ultimately, this affirmation reinforces my understanding that I am worthy of respect and kindness, which is essential for building meaningful relationships and living a fulfilling life.

I take time for self-reflection.

I affirm my commitment to understanding myself better and growing personally. This belief empowers me to pause and evaluate my thoughts, feelings, and experiences, allowing me to gain insight into my motivations and actions.

By prioritizing self-reflection, I cultivate greater self-awareness and clarity, enabling me to make informed decisions that align with my values and goals. This mindset encourages me to learn from my experiences, fostering continuous growth and improvement.

Ultimately, this affirmation reinforces my understanding that taking time for self-reflection is essential for my well-being and personal development, helping me navigate life with intention and purpose.

I am dedicated to personal growth.

I affirm my commitment to evolving and becoming the best version of myself. This belief empowers me to embrace learning opportunities and actively seek out experiences that challenge and inspire me.

By prioritizing personal growth, I cultivate resilience and adaptability, allowing me to navigate life's challenges with a positive mindset. This dedication encourages me to reflect on my strengths and areas for improvement, fostering a continuous cycle of development.

Ultimately, this affirmation reinforces my understanding that being dedicated to personal growth enhances my overall well-being and fulfillment, enabling me to live a more meaningful and purpose-driven life.

I celebrate the successes of others.

I affirm my commitment to fostering a supportive and uplifting environment. This belief empowers me to recognize and appreciate the achievements of those around me, understanding that their victories do not diminish my own.

By celebrating others' successes, I cultivate a mindset of abundance and positivity, which strengthens my relationships and encourages collaboration. This attitude inspires me to learn from their journeys and share in their joy, creating a sense of community and connection.

Ultimately, this affirmation reinforces my understanding that celebrating the successes of others enriches my own life, allowing me to build meaningful connections and contribute to a culture of encouragement and support.

I have the courage to speak my truth.

I affirm my commitment to authenticity and self-expression. This belief empowers me to share my thoughts, feelings, and experiences honestly, even when it feels challenging or uncomfortable.

By embracing this courage, I cultivate confidence in my voice and the importance of my perspective, allowing me to contribute meaningfully to conversations and relationships. This mindset encourages me to stand up for myself and others, fostering a sense of integrity and connection.

Ultimately, this affirmation reinforces my understanding that speaking my truth not only honors my own experiences but also inspires others to do the same, creating a more open and understanding environment for everyone.

I believe in the power of my voice.

I affirm my conviction that my thoughts and opinions matter. This belief empowers me to express myself confidently and to advocate for what I believe in, knowing that my words can create positive change.

By recognizing the power of my voice, I cultivate a sense of responsibility to use it thoughtfully, inspiring others and contributing to important conversations. This mindset encourages me to share my ideas and experiences, fostering connection and understanding within my community.

Ultimately, this affirmation reinforces my understanding that believing in the power of my voice enhances my impact on the world, allowing me to contribute to a dialogue that promotes growth, awareness, and empowerment for myself and others.

I approach life with curiosity and wonder.

I affirm my commitment to exploring the world with an open mind and a sense of adventure. This belief empowers me to embrace new experiences and seek out knowledge, allowing me to see the beauty and possibility in everyday moments.

By cultivating curiosity and wonder, I foster a mindset of learning and growth, encouraging me to ask questions and discover different perspectives. This approach enhances my appreciation for life, making even ordinary experiences feel exciting and meaningful.

Ultimately, this affirmation reinforces my understanding that approaching life with curiosity and wonder enriches my journey, helping me to connect more deeply with myself and the world around me.

I trust in my ability to learn and grow.

I affirm my belief in my capacity for personal development and resilience. This belief empowers me to embrace challenges as opportunities to expand my knowledge and skills, knowing that each experience contributes to my growth.

By trusting in my ability to learn, I cultivate a positive mindset that encourages me to take risks and step outside my comfort zone. This mindset helps me to view setbacks as valuable lessons rather than failures, reinforcing my commitment to continuous improvement.

Ultimately, this affirmation reinforces my understanding that trusting in my ability to learn and grow enables me to navigate life's journey with confidence and optimism, fostering a lifelong love of learning.

I am open to new perspectives.

I affirm my commitment to understanding and embracing diverse viewpoints. This belief empowers me to listen actively and consider ideas that differ from my own, fostering a sense of curiosity and respect for others.

By being open to new perspectives, I cultivate flexibility and adaptability, allowing me to grow and learn from the experiences of those around me. This mindset encourages me to engage in meaningful conversations and deepen my connections with others.

Ultimately, this affirmation reinforces my understanding that embracing new perspectives enriches my life, broadening my horizons and helping me navigate the world with empathy and insight.

I contribute positively to the world around me.

I affirm my commitment to making a meaningful impact in my community and beyond. This belief empowers me to take actions that promote kindness, support, and uplift those I encounter.

By focusing on positive contributions, I cultivate a sense of purpose and fulfillment, knowing that my efforts, no matter how small, can create a ripple effect of goodness. This mindset encourages me to engage in acts of service and to be a source of encouragement for others.

Ultimately, this affirmation reinforces my understanding that my contributions, rooted in compassion and positivity, play a vital role in shaping a better world, enriching both my life and the lives of those around me.

I am worthy of my aspirations.

I affirm my belief in my right to pursue my dreams and goals. This belief empowers me to recognize that my desires and ambitions are valid and deserving of attention.

By embracing my worthiness, I cultivate confidence and motivation, allowing me to take meaningful steps toward achieving what I truly want in life. This mindset encourages me to overcome self-doubt and to trust in my abilities to reach my aspirations.

Ultimately, this affirmation reinforces my understanding that believing in my worthiness is essential for manifesting my dreams, enabling me to create a fulfilling and purpose-driven life.

I embrace vulnerability as a strength.

I affirm my belief that being open and honest about my feelings and experiences is a powerful aspect of my personal growth. This belief empowers me to connect more deeply with others and to foster genuine relationships built on trust and understanding.

By embracing vulnerability, I cultivate resilience and authenticity, allowing myself to express my true self without fear of judgment. This mindset encourages me to see challenges as opportunities for growth, knowing that sharing my struggles can inspire and uplift others.

Ultimately, this affirmation reinforces my understanding that vulnerability is not a weakness but a source of strength, enabling me to navigate life with courage and compassion.

I find strength in my community.

I affirm my belief in the power of connection and support that comes from being part of a collective. This belief empowers me to recognize that I am not alone in my journey and that the people around me can provide encouragement, inspiration, and guidance.

By engaging with my community, I cultivate a sense of belonging and shared purpose, which enhances my resilience and motivation. This mindset encourages me to contribute positively to others' lives, knowing that together we can face challenges and celebrate successes.

Ultimately, this affirmation reinforces my understanding that my community is a vital source of strength, helping me grow and thrive while fostering meaningful relationships that enrich my life.

I am grateful for my support system.

I affirm my appreciation for the people who uplift and encourage me in my life. This belief empowers me to recognize the value of having friends, family, and mentors who provide guidance, love, and understanding during both good times and challenges.

By acknowledging my support system, I cultivate a sense of connection and belonging, knowing that I can lean on others when needed. This mindset encourages me to reciprocate that support, fostering deeper relationships and a sense of community.

Ultimately, this affirmation reinforces my understanding that gratitude for my support system enhances my well-being, helping me navigate life's ups and downs with confidence and resilience.

I let go of what no longer serves me.

I affirm my commitment to prioritizing my well-being and personal growth. This belief empowers me to recognize and release habits, relationships, and thoughts that hinder my progress or drain my energy.

By letting go, I create space for new opportunities and positive experiences, allowing me to focus on what truly enriches my life. This mindset encourages me to embrace change and to trust that releasing the old can lead to a more fulfilling future.

Ultimately, this affirmation reinforces my understanding that letting go of what no longer serves me is essential for my emotional and mental health, enabling me to move forward with clarity and purpose.

I am focused on my purpose.

I affirm my commitment to living a meaningful and intentional life. This belief empowers me to clarify my goals and align my actions with what truly matters to me, providing direction and motivation.

By focusing on my purpose, I cultivate a sense of fulfillment and clarity, allowing me to prioritize my time and energy on activities that resonate with my values. This mindset encourages me to overcome distractions and stay committed to my journey.

Ultimately, this affirmation reinforces my understanding that being focused on my purpose enhances my sense of identity and satisfaction, helping me create a life that reflects who I am and what I aspire to achieve.

I am a lifelong seeker of knowledge.

I affirm my commitment to continuous learning and growth. This belief empowers me to embrace curiosity and explore new ideas, skills, and experiences throughout my life.

By valuing knowledge, I cultivate a mindset that encourages me to ask questions, seek answers, and remain open to different perspectives. This dedication enhances my adaptability and enriches my understanding of the world around me.

Ultimately, this affirmation reinforces my understanding that being a lifelong seeker of knowledge not only fuels my personal development but also empowers me to contribute meaningfully to my community and inspire others on their own journeys.

I believe in my vision for the future.

I affirm my confidence in my aspirations and the direction I want to take in life. This belief empowers me to create a clear picture of my goals and dreams, motivating me to take actionable steps toward achieving them.

By believing in my vision, I cultivate resilience and determination, allowing me to stay focused even when faced with challenges. This mindset encourages me to remain committed to my path and to trust in my ability to bring my dreams to fruition.

Ultimately, this affirmation reinforces my understanding that believing in my vision for the future is essential for my personal fulfillment, guiding me toward a life that aligns with my true self and aspirations.

I take pride in my authenticity.

I affirm my commitment to being true to myself and expressing my genuine thoughts and feelings. This belief empowers me to embrace my unique qualities and to live in a way that reflects my true values and beliefs.

By taking pride in my authenticity, I cultivate confidence and self-acceptance, allowing me to engage with others honestly and openly. This mindset encourages me to foster deeper connections and build relationships based on trust and respect.

Ultimately, this affirmation reinforces my understanding that my authenticity is a source of strength, enabling me to navigate life with integrity and to inspire others to embrace their true selves as well.

I cultivate resilience in myself.

I affirm my commitment to developing the strength to bounce back from challenges and setbacks. This belief empowers me to view difficulties as opportunities for growth, allowing me to learn valuable lessons from my experiences.

By nurturing resilience, I build confidence in my ability to navigate life's ups and downs. This mindset encourages me to remain adaptable and persistent, knowing that I can overcome obstacles and emerge stronger.

Ultimately, this affirmation reinforces my understanding that cultivating resilience is essential for my emotional well-being, enabling me to face challenges with courage and determination while staying focused on my goals.

I inspire others to be their best selves.

I affirm my belief in the positive impact I can have on those around me. This belief empowers me to lead by example, sharing my journey and values in a way that motivates others to pursue their own growth and aspirations.

By striving to inspire, I cultivate a sense of purpose and fulfillment, knowing that my actions and words can encourage others to realize their potential. This mindset encourages me to create a supportive environment where people feel empowered to be their authentic selves.

Ultimately, this affirmation reinforces my understanding that inspiring others not only enriches their lives but also deepens my own sense of connection and purpose, creating a ripple effect of positivity in the world.

I am proactive in creating my future.

I affirm my commitment to taking charge of my life and making intentional choices that align with my goals. This belief empowers me to envision the future I desire and to take actionable steps toward achieving it.

By being proactive, I cultivate a sense of agency and responsibility, allowing me to anticipate challenges and seek solutions rather than waiting for circumstances to change. This mindset encourages me to embrace opportunities and to continuously adapt my plans as needed.

Ultimately, this affirmation reinforces my understanding that being proactive in creating my future enables me to shape my path with confidence and purpose, leading to a fulfilling and meaningful life.

I trust in my journey, no matter the pace.

I affirm my belief that my personal growth and progress unfold in their own time. This belief empowers me to embrace my unique path, recognizing that everyone's journey is different and that there is no one-size-fits-all timeline.

By trusting in my journey, I cultivate patience and self-compassion, allowing me to celebrate small victories and learn from challenges without feeling rushed. This mindset encourages me to focus on my experiences and insights, rather than comparing myself to others.

Ultimately, this affirmation reinforces my understanding that trusting in my journey—regardless of the pace—enables me to move forward with confidence, finding joy and meaning in each step I take.

I am passionate about my interests.

I affirm my enthusiasm and dedication to the things that truly inspire me. This belief empowers me to explore my hobbies and pursuits with excitement, allowing me to invest my time and energy into what I love.

By embracing my passions, I cultivate a sense of fulfillment and joy that enriches my life. This mindset encourages me to seek out opportunities for growth and connection within these areas, deepening my knowledge and skills.

Ultimately, this affirmation reinforces my understanding that being passionate about my interests enhances my well-being and fuels my creativity, helping me to lead a more vibrant and meaningful life.

I recognize my worth and value.

I affirm my belief in my inherent dignity and the unique contributions I bring to the world. This belief empowers me to appreciate my strengths, qualities, and experiences, allowing me to stand confidently in who I am.

By acknowledging my worth, I cultivate self-respect and self-acceptance, which encourages me to set healthy boundaries and pursue opportunities that align with my values.

Ultimately, this affirmation reinforces my understanding that recognizing my worth and value is essential for my overall well-being, enabling me to navigate life with confidence and a sense of purpose.

I am determined to make a difference.

I affirm my commitment to creating positive change in my life and the lives of others. This belief empowers me to take action, whether through small gestures or larger initiatives, knowing that my efforts can have a meaningful impact.

By focusing on making a difference, I cultivate a sense of purpose and motivation that drives me to contribute to my community and beyond. This mindset encourages me to be proactive, seek opportunities for growth, and inspire others to join me in making a positive change.

Ultimately, this affirmation reinforces my understanding that my determination to make a difference not only enriches my own life but also helps foster a sense of connection and hope in the world around me.

I approach each day with intention.

I affirm my commitment to living mindfully and purposefully. This belief empowers me to start each day with a clear focus on my goals and values, allowing me to prioritize what truly matters.

By approaching my days with intention, I cultivate a sense of direction and motivation, making deliberate choices that align with my aspirations. This mindset encourages me to be present in each moment, appreciating the journey rather than just the destination.

Ultimately, this affirmation reinforces my understanding that living with intention enriches my life, helping me to create meaningful experiences and achieve a sense of fulfillment in everything I do.

I celebrate my progress, no matter how small.

I affirm my belief in the importance of recognizing and appreciating every step I take toward my goals. This belief empowers me to acknowledge my achievements, regardless of their size, fostering a sense of accomplishment and motivation.

By celebrating my progress, I cultivate a positive mindset that encourages me to keep moving forward, reinforcing my commitment to continuous growth. This mindset helps me to appreciate the journey and stay motivated, even during challenging times.

Ultimately, this affirmation reinforces my understanding that celebrating my progress enhances my self-confidence and resilience, enabling me to embrace each moment as a valuable part of my path.

I am a source of positivity and light.

I affirm my commitment to spreading joy and optimism in the world around me. This belief empowers me to uplift others through my words, actions, and attitude, creating an environment that encourages hope and inspiration.

By embodying positivity, I cultivate resilience and a sense of fulfillment, knowing that my energy can influence those I interact with. This mindset encourages me to focus on the good, even in challenging situations, and to be a beacon of support for others.

Ultimately, this affirmation reinforces my understanding that being a source of positivity and light not only enhances my own well-being but also fosters meaningful connections and a sense of community among those around me.

I believe in my ability to create change.

I affirm my confidence in my power to influence my life and the world around me. This belief empowers me to take action, knowing that my efforts can lead to meaningful transformations, both big and small.

By trusting in my ability to create change, I cultivate a proactive mindset that encourages me to identify opportunities for improvement and to pursue them with determination. This perspective inspires me to embrace challenges as chances for growth and to motivate others to join in creating positive change.

Ultimately, this affirmation reinforces my understanding that believing in my ability to create change is essential for my personal development, helping me to shape a future that aligns with my values and aspirations.

I am worthy of love and acceptance.

I affirm my belief in my inherent value as a person. This belief empowers me to embrace my uniqueness and recognize that I deserve kindness and compassion from myself and others.

By acknowledging my worthiness, I cultivate self-acceptance and confidence, allowing me to build healthier relationships and set boundaries that honor my needs. This mindset encourages me to let go of self-doubt and embrace vulnerability, knowing that I am deserving of genuine connection.

Ultimately, this affirmation reinforces my understanding that being worthy of love and acceptance is fundamental to my emotional well-being, helping me to create a supportive environment where I can thrive and be my true self.

I am open to growth and transformation.

I affirm my willingness to embrace change and evolve as a person. This belief empowers me to view challenges and new experiences as opportunities for learning, helping me to expand my horizons and enhance my skills.

By being open to growth, I cultivate a mindset of curiosity and resilience, allowing me to adapt to life's ups and downs with confidence. This perspective encourages me to seek out feedback, take risks, and explore different paths that lead to my personal development.

Ultimately, this affirmation reinforces my understanding that being open to growth and transformation is essential for my journey, enabling me to become the best version of myself and to live a fulfilling and meaningful life.

I prioritize my mental health and well-being.

I affirm my commitment to taking care of my emotional and psychological needs. This belief empowers me to recognize the importance of self-care and to make choices that support my overall health.

By prioritizing my mental well-being, I cultivate resilience and clarity, allowing me to navigate challenges more effectively. This mindset encourages me to engage in practices that promote balance, such as mindfulness, exercise, and connecting with supportive people.

Ultimately, this affirmation reinforces my understanding that prioritizing my mental health is essential for my happiness and success, enabling me to lead a more fulfilling and enriched life.

I am capable of balancing my responsibilities.

I affirm my confidence in managing various aspects of my life effectively. This belief empowers me to prioritize my tasks and commitments, allowing me to create a sense of order and stability.

By recognizing my capability, I cultivate a proactive mindset that encourages me to set boundaries and allocate my time wisely. This perspective helps me to avoid feeling overwhelmed and to approach my responsibilities with a sense of purpose and focus.

Ultimately, this affirmation reinforces my understanding that I can find harmony in my life, enabling me to fulfill my obligations while also making time for self-care and personal growth.

I embrace life's uncertainties with grace.

I affirm my willingness to accept the unpredictability of life. This belief empowers me to approach challenges and changes with an open heart and a positive mindset, rather than resisting or fearing them.

By embracing uncertainty, I cultivate resilience and adaptability, allowing me to navigate unexpected situations with confidence. This perspective encourages me to find opportunities for growth in every circumstance, viewing each twist and turn as a chance to learn and evolve.

Ultimately, this affirmation reinforces my understanding that embracing life's uncertainties enriches my experiences, helping me to live fully and authentically, even amidst the unknown.

I nurture my relationships with love and care.

I affirm my commitment to fostering meaningful connections with others. This belief empowers me to invest time and energy into the people who matter most in my life, ensuring that our bonds grow stronger and deeper.

By nurturing my relationships, I cultivate empathy and understanding, allowing me to communicate openly and supportively. This mindset encourages me to show appreciation and kindness, creating a positive and loving environment for everyone involved.

Ultimately, this affirmation reinforces my understanding that nurturing my relationships enriches my life and the lives of those around me, helping us to build a supportive community where we can thrive together.

I am committed to being my best self.

I believe that personal growth and self-improvement lead to a more fulfilling life.

By striving to better myself, I can positively impact those around me and contribute to my community. I recognize that this journey requires dedication, self-reflection, and resilience, but I am motivated by the desire to embrace new challenges, learn from my experiences, and cultivate meaningful relationships. Ultimately, being my best self not only enhances my own well-being but also allows me to inspire and support others in their journeys.

I am resilient, no matter the circumstance.

I believe in my ability to adapt and overcome challenges.

Life is full of unexpected obstacles, but I have learned that setbacks are opportunities for growth. I draw strength from my experiences, knowing that each struggle has made me more capable and resourceful. My resilience allows me to maintain a positive outlook, stay focused on my goals, and find solutions even in difficult times. I trust in my inner strength and the support of those around me, which empowers me to navigate any situation with confidence.

I find joy in the process, not just the outcome.

I believe that the journey itself holds valuable lessons and experiences.

Each step I take allows me to learn, grow, and discover new aspects of myself. I cherish the small victories and the moments of creativity that come along the way, as they enrich my life and deepen my understanding.

By focusing on the process, I can appreciate the effort and dedication I put in, rather than just the final result. This mindset helps me stay motivated and fulfilled, reminding me that the experience is just as important as the destination.

I have the power to influence my reality.

I understand that my thoughts, actions, and decisions shape my experiences.

By taking responsibility for my choices, I can create the life I desire. I recognize that I can change my perspective and approach challenges with a proactive mindset.

This empowerment motivates me to set goals, embrace opportunities, and take meaningful steps toward my aspirations. I believe that by cultivating a positive attitude and staying true to my values, I can transform my circumstances and manifest the reality I want to live in.

I am deserving of all good things.

I recognize my worth and the value I bring to the world.

I believe that everyone, including myself, has the right to happiness, love, and success. Embracing this belief allows me to open myself up to opportunities and experiences that enrich my life. I acknowledge my efforts and growth, and I understand that I am worthy of the rewards that come from hard work and dedication.

By affirming my deservingness, I cultivate a mindset of abundance and invite positive experiences into my life.

I strive to uplift and empower others.

I believe in the transformative power of support and encouragement.

When I help others recognize their strengths and potential, I contribute to their growth and confidence. I've seen how a kind word, or a listening ear can make a difference, and I want to be a source of positivity in their lives.

By fostering a sense of community and connection, I not only help others thrive but also enrich my own life. Empowering others creates a ripple effect, inspiring everyone to reach their fullest potential.

I embrace the journey of self-discovery.

Each step I take helps me uncover my passions, values, and strengths, guiding me toward a deeper understanding of who I am.

I welcome challenges and new experiences as opportunities to learn and evolve. This journey allows me to reflect on my choices and aspirations, helping me align my life with my true self.

By embracing self-discovery, I not only enhance my own life but also become more open and authentic in my relationships with others.

I am filled with potential and promise.

I believe in my ability to grow and achieve great things.

I recognize that within me lies the capacity to learn, adapt, and overcome challenges. Embracing this mindset motivates me to pursue my goals and dreams with enthusiasm. I understand that every experience, whether positive or negative, contributes to my journey and shapes my future.

By acknowledging my potential, I am inspired to take bold steps forward and create a life that reflects my aspirations and values. This belief empowers me to strive for excellence and make a meaningful impact in the world.

I seek out experiences that enrich my life.

I believe in the power of exploration and growth.

By actively pursuing new adventures, whether through travel, learning, or connecting with diverse people, I expand my horizons and gain valuable insights. These experiences help me discover more about myself and the world around me, fostering creativity and resilience. I cherish the moments that challenge me and push me outside my comfort zone, as they lead to personal development and fulfillment. Ultimately, I strive to fill my life with meaningful experiences that enhance my understanding and appreciation of life.

I practice mindfulness and presence.

By focusing on the present moment, I can fully engage with my experiences and emotions, reducing stress and anxiety. This practice helps me appreciate the small joys in everyday life and fosters a deeper connection with myself and those around me.

Mindfulness allows me to respond to challenges with clarity and calmness rather than reacting impulsively. By cultivating this awareness, I create space for growth, gratitude, and a more meaningful existence.

I am an active participant in my life.

I believe in taking charge of my choices and actions.

I understand that my decisions shape my experiences and that I have the power to create the life I want. By engaging fully in my pursuits and being intentional about my goals, I cultivate a sense of purpose and fulfillment.

I embrace opportunities for growth and learning, knowing that being proactive helps me navigate challenges with resilience. By actively participating in my life, I empower myself to make the most of every moment and contribute positively to the world around me.

I approach challenges with confidence.

I trust in my ability to learn and adapt.

I understand that obstacles are a natural part of life and offer opportunities for growth. By maintaining a positive mindset, I can focus on finding solutions rather than being overwhelmed by difficulties. My past experiences have taught me resilience and resourcefulness, reinforcing my belief that I can overcome any hurdle.

This confidence empowers me to take risks and embrace new experiences, knowing that each challenge I face contributes to my personal development and strength.

I trust in the process of growth.

I recognize that it takes time and effort to develop into the person I aspire to be.

I understand that growth is not always linear and that setbacks can be valuable lessons. By embracing the journey, I allow myself to learn from each experience, celebrating progress along the way.

I believe that patience and perseverance are key, and I find comfort in knowing that every step, no matter how small, brings me closer to my goals. This trust in the process helps me stay motivated and open to new opportunities for personal development.

I find strength in vulnerability.

This affirmation allows me to be authentic and connect deeply with others.

Embracing my emotions and sharing my experiences fosters trust and understanding in my relationships. I've learned that showing vulnerability is not a sign of weakness, but rather a courageous step toward personal growth and healing. It opens the door to meaningful conversations and helps me develop resilience as I navigate challenges.

By accepting my vulnerabilities, I empower myself to embrace my true self and create a supportive environment where others feel safe to do the same.

I am open to receiving love and support.

I recognize that connection and community are vital to my well-being.

Accepting help from others enriches my life and strengthens my relationships. I understand that allowing myself to be vulnerable and letting others in creates a foundation of trust and mutual respect. By being open to love and support, I not only enhance my own experiences but also create space for others to feel valued and appreciated.

This openness fosters a sense of belonging and encourages a positive cycle of giving and receiving in my life.

I recognize my progress over time.

I believe it's important to acknowledge how far I've come in my personal journey.

By reflecting on my experiences, I can see the growth and development that have shaped me. Celebrating my achievements, both big and small, boosts my confidence and motivates me to keep moving forward. I understand that progress isn't always visible day-to-day, but taking the time to appreciate my evolution helps me stay grounded and focused on my goals.

This recognition fosters gratitude for my journey and encourages me to continue striving for improvement.

I am a champion of my own story.

I believe in the power of my experiences and the unique perspective I bring to the world.

I embrace my journey, including the challenges and triumphs, as they have shaped who I am today. By owning my narrative, I empower myself to advocate for my needs and goals, while also inspiring others to do the same. I understand that my voice matters, and sharing my story can foster connection and understanding.

Celebrating my journey allows me to live authentically and courageously, reinforcing my belief that I have the strength to create my own path.

I celebrate the beauty of diversity in others.

I believe that our differences enrich our lives and broaden our perspectives.

Each unique background, culture, and experience adds depth to our interactions and fosters a greater understanding of the world. By embracing diversity, I create an inclusive environment where everyone feels valued and respected. I recognize that learning from others' stories and viewpoints not only enhances my own growth but also strengthens our connections.

Celebrating diversity allows me to appreciate the richness of human experience and inspires me to cultivate empathy and compassion in all my relationships.

I am committed to my personal values.

By staying true to what I believe in, I create a sense of integrity and authenticity that influences my relationships and pursuits. My values serve as a compass, helping me navigate challenges and stay aligned with my goals.

This commitment empowers me to make choices that reflect who I am and what I stand for, fostering a deeper sense of fulfillment. Ultimately, honoring my values allows me to live a life that is meaningful and in harmony with my true self.

I am proud to be the person I am today.

I have worked hard to grow and evolve through my experiences.

Each challenge and triumph have contributed to my character and shaped my values. I embrace my uniqueness and the journey that has led me here, recognizing that my strengths and imperfections make me who I am. This pride fuels my confidence and inspires me to continue striving for personal growth.

I celebrate my progress and the lessons I've learned, knowing that they empower me to create a positive impact in my life and the lives of others.

Printed in the United States
by Baker & Taylor Publisher Services